big & SMALL

Original Korean text and illustrations by Dreaming Tortoise
Korean edition © Aram Publishing

This English edition published by big & SMALL in 2017
by arrangement with Aram Publishing
English text edited by Scott Forbes
English edition © big & SMALL 2017

Distributed in the United States and Canada by
Lerner Publishing Group, Inc.
241 First Avenue North
Minneapolis, MN 55401 U.S.A.
www.lernerbooks.com

Photo credits:
Page 29, top: © Rodney-Perot Museum

ISBN: 978-1-925235-24-1
Printed in Korea

To learn more about dinosaur fossils, see page 28.
For information on the main groups of dinosaurs,
see the Dinosaur Family Tree on page 30.

Three-horned
Triceratops

Triceratops

big & SMALL

Giganotosaurus

SAY IT:
Jye-gan-oh-toh-SAW-rus

A group of Giganotosaurus were on the prowl, hunting for food. They searched through the forest, trying to spot or pick up the scent of prey. But it seemed that there were no other creatures around.

Giganotosaurus means "giant southern lizard," and this was one of the largest of all the meat-eating dinosaurs. Giganotosaurus hunted in groups, or packs. Working together, a pack could capture even the biggest plant-eaters.

Then the Giganotosaurus got lucky. A baby Argentinosaurus was walking around on its own. It had clearly wandered away from the protection of its family group.

The Giganotosaurus closed in on their prey, roaring and baring their long, dagger-like teeth.

ARGENTINOSAURUS

GROUP: Sauropods
DIET: Plants
WHEN IT LIVED: Late Cretaceous
WHERE IT LIVED: South America
(Argentina)
LENGTH: 100–115 feet (30–35 meters)
HEIGHT: 20–26 feet (6–8 meters)
WEIGHT: 77 tons
(70 tonnes)

LENGTH: 40–46 feet
(12–14 meters)

HEIGHT: 23–26 feet
(7–8 meters)

WEIGHT: 6.6–7.7 tons
(6–7 tonnes)

WHEN IT LIVED:	TRIASSIC	JURASSIC	CRETACEOUS

GROUP: Theropods	DIET: Meat

WHERE IT LIVED:
South America
(Argentina)

Triceratops

SAY IT:
Try-SEH-ra-tops

Two Triceratops were grazing on some shrubs.
All of a sudden, a Troodon sped past them.

The Triceratops sensed danger.
What could the Troodon
be running from? They
looked around anxiously.

The name "Triceratops" means "three-horned face." Triceratops' horns and its huge neck frill helped protect its head. Its jaws were a bit like a giant parrot's beak, and were strong enough to rip up the toughest plants. Triceratops would then use its broad back teeth to mash the plant pieces into a pulp.

TROODON

GROUP: Theropods
DIET: Meat
WHEN IT LIVED: Late Cretaceous
WHERE IT LIVED: North America
(USA, Canada)
LENGTH: 5–6.6 feet (1.5–2 meters)
HEIGHT: 4 feet (1.2 meters)
WEIGHT: 110 pounds
(50 kilograms)

HEIGHT: **10 feet**
(3 meters)

LENGTH: **26–30 feet**
(8–9 meters)

WEIGHT: **8.8 tons**
(8 tonnes)

WHEN IT LIVED:	TRIASSIC	JURASSIC	CRETACEOUS

GROUP: **Ceratopsians**	DIET: **Plants**

WHERE IT LIVED:
North America
(USA, Canada)

11

The Triceratops realized what was happening.
A Tyrannosaurus was thundering toward them!

The Triceratops did not turn and run.
Instead, they stood firm and pointed their huge
horns toward their foe. Often the sight of those
spear-like horns would be enough to make a
meat-eater think twice about attacking.

TYRANNOSAURUS

GROUP: Theropods
DIET: Meat
WHEN IT LIVED: Late Cretaceous
WHERE IT LIVED: North America
(USA, Canada)
LENGTH: 40–43 feet (12–13 meters)
HEIGHT: 20 feet (6 meters)
WEIGHT: 6.6–7.7 tons
(6–7 tonnes)

Triceratops roamed the plains, feeding on low plants.
They traveled in large groups, or herds. When under
attack, the adults would steer their young into the
middle of the herd to protect them.

Young Triceratops used their horns to fight each other.
Sometimes this was just for play. But they also fought
for real over female Triceratops.

Maiasaura

SAY IT:
My-ah-SAW-rah

There was a cracking sound and one of the eggs broke open. A tiny Maiasaura crawled out of the shell. Then another egg broke open and a second baby dinosaur appeared.

The mother watched her babies closely. She had food ready for them. As more babies appeared, she looked around, watching for any creatures that might steal her young.

GROUP: Theropods
DIET: Plants and meat
WHEN IT LIVED: Late Cretaceous
WHERE IT LIVED: North America
(USA, Canada), Asia (China)
LENGTH: 13 feet (4 meters)
HEIGHT: 6.6 feet (2 meters)
WEIGHT: 770 pounds
(350 kilograms)

Maiasaura means "good mother reptile." Most dinosaurs laid their eggs on open ground and then left them to hatch on their own. But the mother Maiasaura laid her eggs in a nest, stayed close to the nest until the eggs hatched, and then kept watch over her babies until they were strong enough to fend for themselves.

LENGTH: 30 feet
(9 meters)

HEIGHT: 10–13 feet
(3–4 meters)

WEIGHT: 3.3 tons
(3 tonnes)

WHEN IT LIVED:	TRIASSIC	JURASSIC	CRETACEOUS

GROUP: Ornithopods	DIET: Plants

WHERE IT LIVED:
North America
(USA, Canada)

15

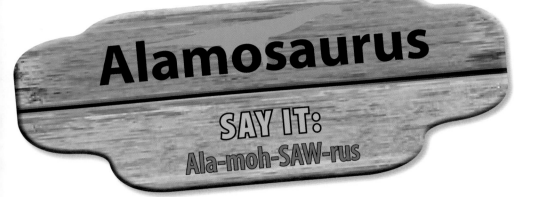

Alamosaurus

A group of giant Alamosaurus were splashing about in a shallow lake, enjoying the warm sun and cool water. Overhead, a Quetzalcoatlus, a huge flying reptile, swooped across the treetops.

HEIGHT: 20 feet
(6 meters)

LENGTH: 66 feet
(20 meters)

WEIGHT: 33 tons
(30 tonnes)

WHEN IT LIVED: TRIASSIC | JURASSIC | CRETACEOUS

GROUP: Sauropods

DIET: Plants

WHERE IT LIVED:
North America
(USA)

The Alamosaurus spotted a couple of Tyrannosaurus at the water's edge. They lumbered out of the water and gathered together to face the fierce meat-eaters. They were determined to keep them away from their young. Could they hold the Tyrannosaurus at bay?

For protection against meat-eating dinosaurs, Alamosaurus moved around in large herds. They tried to keep their young in the middle of the herd to protect them from danger.

QUETZALCOATLUS

GROUP: Pterosaurs
DIET: Meat
WHEN IT LIVED: Late Cretaceous
WHERE IT LIVED: North America
(USA)
WINGSPAN: 36–40 feet (11–12 meters)
HEIGHT: 10 feet (3 meters)
WEIGHT: 200 pounds
(90 kilograms)

TYRANNOSAURUS

GROUP: Theropods
DIET: Meat
WHEN IT LIVED: Late Cretaceous
WHERE IT LIVED: North America
(USA, Canada)
LENGTH: 40–43 feet (12–13 meters)
HEIGHT: 20 feet (6 meters)
WEIGHT: 6.6–7.7 tons
(6–7 tonnes)

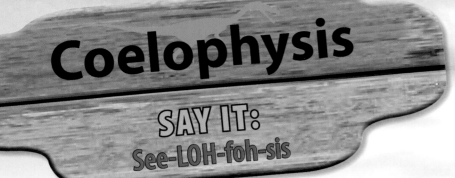

Coelophysis

With a sudden lunge of its long neck, a
Coelophysis snatched up a passing lizard.
Other Coelophysis gathered around,
eyeing the lizard enviously.
They were all hungry.
They needed to find
more food.

20

Coelophysis was among the earliest dinosaurs. Its name means "hollow form," and it was given that name because its bones were hollow. This made Coelophysis' body very light, which in turn helped it run fast.

The herd of Coelophysis spotted a Postosuchus coming out of a nearby pond. They darted toward it, snarling and hissing. Even though the Postosuchus was much larger than them, the Coelophysis began to attack it from all sides. Soon they had brought it to the ground. There would be plenty to eat now!

POSTOSUCHUS

GROUP: Reptiles
DIET: Meat
WHEN IT LIVED: Late Triassic
WHERE IT LIVED: North America
(USA)
LENGTH: 13–16 feet (4–5 meters)
HEIGHT: 6.6 feet (2 meters)
WEIGHT: 660–880 pounds
(300-700 kilograms)

Partly because it had such a light and slender body, Coelophysis could survive for a long time without food or water. Unlike many dinosaurs, its eyes were close together and faced forward, so it could also see very well.

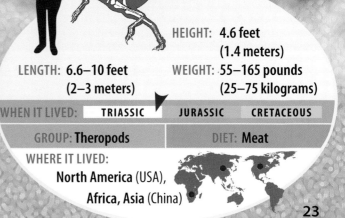

LENGTH: 6.6–10 feet (2–3 meters)

HEIGHT: 4.6 feet (1.4 meters)

WEIGHT: 55–165 pounds (25–75 kilograms)

WHEN IT LIVED:	TRIASSIC	JURASSIC	CRETACEOUS

GROUP: Theropods	DIET: Meat

WHERE IT LIVED:
North America (USA), Africa, Asia (China)

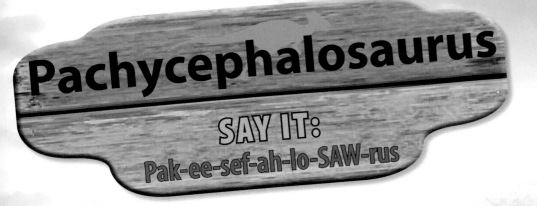

Pachycephalosaurus

SAY IT:
Pak-ee-sef-ah-lo-SAW-rus

The young male Pachycephalosaurus had been shoving and jostling each other for some time. Each was determined to show the other that he was stronger.

EDMONTOSAURUS

GROUP: Ornithopods
DIET: Plants
WHEN IT LIVED: Late Cretaceous
WHERE IT LIVED: North America
(USA, Canada)
LENGTH: 43 feet (13 meters)
HEIGHT: 16 feet (5 meters)
WEIGHT: 3.3–4.4 tons
(3–4 tonnes)

LENGTH: 13–16 feet
(4–5 meters)

HEIGHT: 6.6 feet
(2 meters)

WEIGHT: 550–660 pounds
(250–300 kilograms)

WHEN IT LIVED: TRIASSIC JURASSIC CRETACEOUS

GROUP: Pachycephalosaurs

DIET: Plants

WHERE IT LIVED:
North America
(Canada), Asia
(South Korea)

The Pachycephalosaurus then placed their heads together and began pushing and butting each other. Every so often, one of them would give way and back off. But then they would start all over again.

They were so caught up in their battle that they didn't even notice a dangerous Tyrannosaurus approaching. Would they realize in time to turn and flee?

Pachycephalosaurus means "thick-headed lizard." The top of this dinosaur's skull was very thick. It almost looked like it was wearing a helmet! Male Pachycephalosaurus had thicker skulls than females, probably because they regularly butted their heads together in battles of strength.

TYRANNOSAURUS

GROUP: Theropods
DIET: Meat
WHEN IT LIVED: Late Cretaceous
WHERE IT LIVED: North America
(USA, Canada)
LENGTH: 40–43 feet (12–13 meters)
HEIGHT: 20 feet (6 meters)
WEIGHT: 6.6–7.7 tons
(6–7 tonnes)

Dinosaur Fossils

Fossils are the remains of dinosaurs. They can be hard parts of dinosaurs, such as bones and teeth, that have slowly turned to stone. Or they may be impressions of bones, teeth, or skin preserved in rocks.

▲ Model of a Giganotosaurus skeleton

Giganotosaurus

It was a car mechanic and amateur fossil hunter called Ruben Carolini who found the first Giganotosaurus fossils, in Argentina, South America, in 1993. Scientists later showed that Giganotosaurus was related to giant meat-eaters in other continents, including Carcharodontosaurus in Africa and Acrocanthosaurus in North America.

Triceratops

Triceratops fossils were first discovered in Denver, in Colorado, USA, in 1887. They were sent to a famous dinosaur hunter, Othniel Marsh, who gave the dinosaur its name, meaning "three-horned face." In the early 1900s, another famous dinosaur hunter, Barnum Brown, collected lots of Triceratops fossils at a place called Hell Creek in Montana, USA, and claimed to have seen hundreds of three-horned skulls there. Triceratops fossils have since been found in other parts of the USA and in Canada.

▲ Model of a Triceratops skeleton

Maiasaura

▲ Re-creation of a Maiasaura nest, with eggs and babies

In 1978, an American dinosaur expert, Jack Horner, discovered the tiny bones of 15 baby dinosaurs surrounded by fossilized egg shells. He realized this was the nest of a previously unknown dinosaur. Further studies revealed that the babies had stayed in the nest for some time after birth, where their mother had clearly fed and cared for them. So Horner named the new species Maiasaura, meaning "good mother lizard."

Alamosaurus

Fossils of Alamosaurus were first discovered in the desert of New Mexico, in the United States, in 1921. The dinosaur was named by Charles Whitney Gilmore for a nearby trading post called Ojo Alamo. More fossils were found across the southwestern United States and scientists gradually realized that this was probably the biggest dinosaur that had ever lived in North America. It may even have been as big as South America's famous Argentinosaurus, one of the biggest dinosaurs of all time.

▲ Model of Alamosaurus skeleton, Perot Museum, Dallas, USA

Coelophysis

In 1881, an amateur fossil hunter, David Baldwin, found the first Coelophysis fossils in New Mexico, in the southwestern United States. The fossils were not identified until 1889, when dinosaur expert Edward Drinker Cope gave them the name Coelophysis. In 1947, a remarkable discovery of hundreds of complete Coelophysis fossils was made at Ghost Ranch, New Mexico. It's thought that a sudden flood or a drought may have caused all of these dinosaurs to have died in the same place at the same time.

▲ Model of skeletons of Coelophysis adult and young

Pachycephalosaurus

Fossils of Pachycephalosaurus were dug up by an amateur collector, Ferdinand Hayden, in Montana, USA, in the early 1850s. But the dinosaur was not named until 1931, after a skull was found in Wyoming, USA. Other examples of this dinosaur's thick skull were found by dinosaur hunter Barnum Brown in 1943. Scientists now think that Pachycephalosaurus' thick skull was used partly for display – in other words, to attract females.

▲ Model of a Pachycephalosaurus skull

201 MILLION YEARS AGO

THE DINOSAUR FAMILY TREE

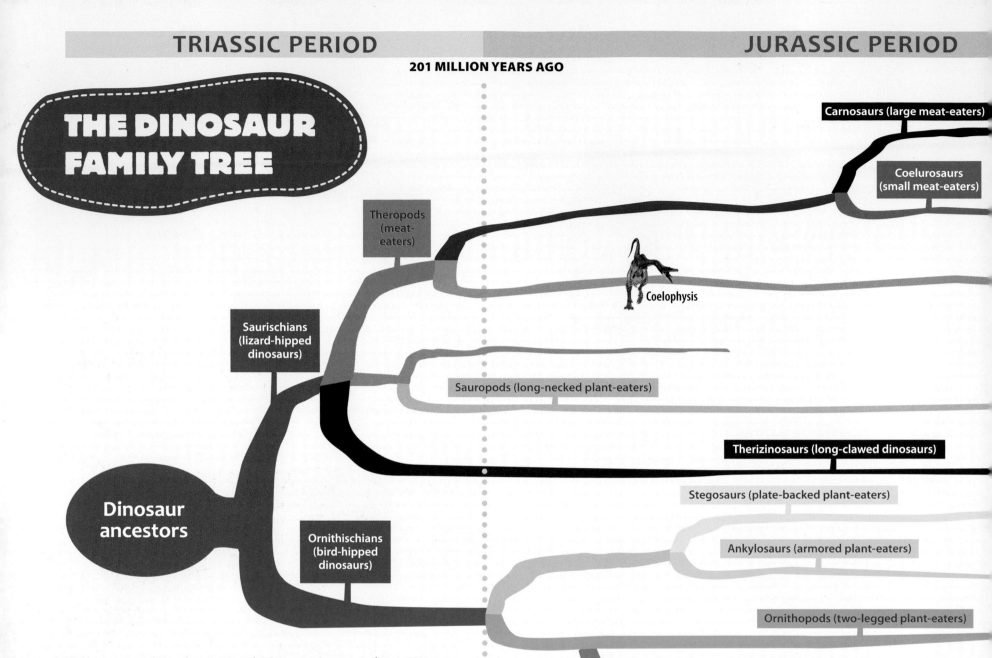

Carnosaurs (large meat-eaters)

Coelurosaurs (small meat-eaters)

Theropods (meat-eaters)

Coelophysis

Saurischians (lizard-hipped dinosaurs)

Sauropods (long-necked plant-eaters)

Therizinosaurs (long-clawed dinosaurs)

Stegosaurs (plate-backed plant-eaters)

Dinosaur ancestors

Ankylosaurs (armored plant-eaters)

Ornithischians (bird-hipped dinosaurs)

Ornithopods (two-legged plant-eaters)

Dinosaurs lived on Earth from about 245 million years ago until about 66 million years ago — long before the first humans. After the first dinosaurs appeared, they spread to all the continents and many different kinds of dinosaurs emerged. This chart shows the main groups of dinosaurs.

Pterosaurs (flying reptiles)

Ichthyosaurs (marine reptiles)

Postosuchus